KU-215-697

Arnold Benington

Adventures of an Ulster Naturalist

Foreword by Michael Benington

Selected, edited and with an afterword
by Jonathan Benington

Dedicated to the memory of Fiona (Woney) and Nicky

Cover: Unknown photographer, Arnold Benington and Hushwing at the
BBC, 1947

Inside front cover: Arnold Benington, Self-portrait photographing rook's
nest, 1923

Published by Brown's Fine Art Ltd. 2009

Supported by the A E Harvey Charitable Trust

Text and images copyright © Michael Benington

ISBN 978-0-9559727-1-3

Printed by Emtone in a limited edition of 500 copies www.emtone.co.uk

Design by Ninepoint www.ninepoint.co.uk

Contents

Foreword by Michael Benington

It is a long-standing Quaker tradition that children should be educated in the appreciation and understanding of natural history. Hence Charles Benington, headmaster of Brookfield School near Moira, saw to it that his son Arnold was introduced very early to the mysteries and joys of the natural world.

Arnold soon realised that careful observation in the field was great fun and a good basis for developing his new interests. Further help was provided when Horace G. Alexander visited Brookfield and gave him his first bird books and good advice on birdwatching skills (H. G. was not only a very influential Quaker but also a highly respected ornithologist).

With time on his hands and help and advice from sympathetic adults, Arnold began to explore the rural environs of his home and to develop an approach that would stand him in good stead in years to come. Early on in his childhood he conquered a fear of heights and acquired a real taste for adventure as he climbed trees and cliffs in search of birds' nests. This moulded a character who in adulthood would be physically very energetic, mentally determined, single-minded, resourceful and caring.

Coming from a family tradition of teaching, he pursued a career path that led him to read chemistry at Queen's University, Belfast. Here he played hockey for their First Eleven and met a small group of like-minded men who remained his friends and fellow adventurers into old age.

Diary-keeping, started as a boy, was developed as a means of recording his now expanding fieldwork – he left over two dozen diaries with detailed accounts of his doings.

After graduation Arnold taught briefly in England, and then in 1927 a vacancy for a science master became available nearer home. His interview with the headmaster at Friends School in Lisburn was abruptly interrupted by

Charles Benington, Brookfield School near Moira, 1920s (now falling into ruin)

an excited Arnold leaping from his chair in mid-question as he glimpsed a sparowhawk taking a blackbird from the lawn outside. Thankfully a perceptive head treated the episode as an example of the sort of enthusiasm he needed in his school!

Quickly established in Friends School, Arnold took over hockey coaching, with brilliant results[1], in addition to running the natural history society. The latter became famous for its end of term 'conversazione', which climaxed when a side wall of his laboratory blossomed into a papier mâché cliff covered in guillemots and other sea birds, all lent from the Ulster Museum's taxidermy collection.

1. One team member, Steven Johnson, was chosen for the British hockey squad at the 1956 Melbourne Olympics.

Other school activities involved reading to boarders, at lights-out, from one of Zane Grey's western novels – a favourite author for his own leisure! His sense of humour and mischief was directed at scripting and producing Irish comedy plays derived from Lynn Doyle stories. These were way over the top and vied to bring the house down, almost literally!

Despite the wartime evacuation of Friends School to Dunmurry, Arnold's natural history work was pursued through field trips to sites close to home, and often to Rathlin Island, one of his favourite haunts (undeterred by not owning a car, he would cycle the 60 miles from Lisburn to Ballycastle). In his 'spare' time he branched out into lecture tours around the province, illustrated with his own slides. He also launched himself as a journalist and began a separate broadcasting career on Children's Hour, regularly linking up with the BBC's natural history unit in Bristol and other naturalists such as Sir Peter Scott.

On retirement from teaching in 1968, Arnold could look back on a life devoted to educating children and adults, to landmark studies on sparrowhawks, to two expeditions to the remote interior of Iceland, and to a lead role in establishing Northern Ireland's first Bird Observatory (it continues his work to this day).

The selection of stories that follows spans half a century and falls into three sections – field diaries, broadcasts and articles. They include both serious missions and light-hearted accounts evincing an awareness of how the uninitiated may have viewed him. I was privileged to have accompanied Arnold on many of these expeditions. Their re-telling will hopefully disseminate the inspirational passion for nature and thirst for adventure that constituted his legacy to me.

Arnold Benington, Flowers of Norway Maple, 1929

Arnold Benington, Leveret, 1936

Field diaries

Arnold Benington, Peregrine chicks, 6 June 1936

Peregrine eyrie in the Mournes; field diary entry 1939[2]

I had a grand day in the Mournes with the Senior Natural History Society people [from Friends School]. The Head gave us the day off and we started about 9.30 in three of Thompson's Taxis.

I had carefully warned them beforehand about coming in unsuitable clothing, but was not fully prepared to see such a tough looking crowd as gathered in the Lab to check up before starting. All my old clothing that I keep in a store cupboard in the Lab for emergencies, had been commissioned ... I had said "old clothing" was to be worn; but they had gone one better and only produced the oldest! They looked rather like a party of Albanian brigands, and enjoyed it! But the pièce de résistance was certainly Corbett's trousers. I had lent him an old gardening pair of mine, long since passed out of existence as trousers, and getting into the taxi they had caught on the door and ripped from knee to ankle – quite a long way with Corbett (by the way) as he is 5 ft 11 inches in height. Nothing loath, he produced a piece of sticking plaster and stuck the seam the whole way up; not exactly an invisible mend. The result had to be seen to be believed! ...

By 11.15 we were tramping up the stony valley towards the [Hare's] Gap. The day was fine with good cloud effects on the mountains, and our spirits rose high. No wheatears were seen this year and the butterwort was not yet in bloom. Corbett, Haughton, Honeyford and I deviated from the path for a few minutes to take a photograph by the stream, and while we were there a peregrine called once (not the alarm note, but a wailing cry) from the slate cliffs of Spellack. Several pairs of stonechat allowed of a close approach with the binoculars, and in so doing called forth exclamations of wonder at their brilliant colouring.

The Gap was reached about 12.20. I took a photograph here of the party sitting on a wall, gazing up at the mountains, and hope it will be a success because the setting was beautiful. We now had a council of war, and in a few minutes decided to hide the heavy rope, and cases for tea etc. in a secluded crevice, and to start immediately afterwards on an ascent of Bearnagh. Halfway up we had lunch on a convenient plateau among the heather and rough grasses, and quite close to the big wall. This was a place we were to remember on our way down again.

After an almost too hearty lunch, for an enterprise like ours, we set our faces upwards again and made surprisingly good time in spite of everything. Following a

---

2 Nature Diary, unpublished manuscript, 20 May 1939

Unknown photographer, Raven's nest, on our way, 14 March 1936 steep climb we arrived at the jagged summit about two o'clock, and had good fun scrambling over the interesting crags in an attempt to find out which of the tops was the top.

Corbett, Haughton, Helene, Sheila and Heather Johnston posed on the summit for a moment while I tried a photograph. A mist came over now and blotted out everything except the immediate surroundings, and as we stared into the wet grey blanket, the deep note of a raven sounded from somewhere close at hand. I told my companions to keep quiet, and presently a large black form glided silently out of the mist and sailed past quite close to us. But in a moment it was gone again, swallowed up by the twisting wraiths of mist, and only the deep "arrrk, aarrrk!" floated back to remind us of the passing of this sable hunter of the crags.

Before starting the descent the mist lifted momentarily and gave us a magnificent view. From our vantage point we saw the following loughs – Shannagh, Binnian lough and Bearnagh blue lough, and of course all the northerly peaks were clearly visible:- Donard, Commedagh, Slievenaglogh, Meelmore, Ben Crom, Binnian, Lamagan, Cove Mountain, Slieve Beg and others.

On the way down it began to rain and got worse until we had to take shelter, such as it was, under the Water Commissioner's wall, close to the little plateau where we had lunch on the ascent. Here we got very wet but the children kept cheerful, and by three o'clock it began to improve. So we continued downwards in a steady drizzle, collected our hidden belongings at the Hare's Gap, and in spite of soaking heather began our search for the peregrine. Edwards, Honeyford, Haughton and I searched the cliffs thoroughly near the old site. But we drew a complete blank and started downwards with the rest of the party.

We now remembered hearing a peregrine call from Spellack on our way up the valley, and considered the possibility of its having deserted the old site in favour of a new one. … When we came to the foot of the huge rock that rises steeply out of the floor of the valley I called a halt. Most of the girls and some of the boys had got very wet, so I thought it wiser to send them on down to the farm, where with the aid of a huge turf fire they would get well warmed and dried. The others were keen to make the attempt on the rock with me, so as soon as we had seen the soaked ones off we crossed over the stream and began to climb.

Now the fun began. A pair of peregrines leapt into the air overhead screaming and I knew at once that my "hunch" was correct; that somewhere ahead and above us was the eyrie. In many ways this was the most enjoyable part of the day. We felt that our goal was in sight, but our difficulty was to locate the nest on a huge unknown cliff face, in the short time at our disposal.

Arrived at the foot of the crag we split up. Norman [Greeves] who had joined us by arrangement at the Hare's Gap about 8.45, went to the left with Jakob, Helene and Edwards, while I took to the right with Corbett, Henning, Honeyford, Glass and Angela. The front face of the cliff was sheer so we did not attempt it as there was no time for ropework. Our method was to climb upwards in easy stages from ledge to ledge, working along each ledge in turn horizontally until we could get no further round the face. Then we traversed back to the starting point and climbed up onto the next ledge; and so on.

And all the time we kept a sharp lookout for droppings, feathers, bones, castings – anything that we thought would give an indication of the whereabouts of our

Michael Benington, Peregrine, 1989

objective. On many of the heather-clad ledges birds had been plucked, and we found many feathers of pigeon and snipe, but no other sign of the eyrie. We were gradually approaching the top now. Up and up we went – slowly and carefully – and determined to see the nest if it could be seen from our side. Norman had called that it was not to be seen anywhere on their part of the cliff, and we were beginning to think that we should soon be forced to make a similar declaration. Time was flying, and we were nearly as high as we could get.

However we managed to get up another four feet and work carefully outwards along a rather narrow ledge. I had ideal companions here, for Honeyford and Corbett were cool as cucumbers on the dizziest heights, and very cheerful in spite of the shockingly wet condition of the heather and rough grasses.

The find of a falcon's primary feather here made us even keener to bring the hunt to a satisfactory conclusion, and as Corbett was putting this into a box for me I worked round a shoulder of rock and shouted "Here's the nest! I've found the peregrine's nest with young!" What excitement then prevailed. The others came hurrying as fast as conditions permitted, in our direction shouting "Where?" Jakob told me afterwards that when he heard my shout "it went right through me."

With the exercise of great care, and our binoculars, everybody got a good view of the four downy young on a ledge about forty feet below us. It would have been foolish to attempt to get at the eyrie without the rope, and we had left it at the foot of the cliff. No time to go back for it now either, so after another look we turned downwards. What a lookout the peregrine had from this ledge! The grandeur of the view impressed us as the floor of the valley swept away apparently thousands of feet below. And it was down this valley we went, to join the others before a roaring fire, where our tale was told and numerous sandwiches devoured.

First buzzard in Ireland, Rathlin; field diary entry 1949[3]

Penned in Bull Lighthouse, Rathlin, during visit with George Nash and Michael Benington.

Gradually returned to consciousness about 7.00 a.m. and managed to hit the floor by 7.15, and ruefully fingering my chin decided that I must shave. Managed that in half a pint of cold water (as all the water has to be carried).

Arnold Benington, A sea cave on Rathlin – chough and rock dove's habitat

---

3 Rathlin Survey, unpublished manuscript, entries for 9 and 12 July 1949. Since then, Buzzards have rapidly spread west and now occur all the way to Donegal.

Gordon Greeves, Rathlin expedition, May 1952
left to right: Arnold Benington, Michael Benington, Jack Miller, Colin Evans, Reggie Perry, Brian Perry, Tommy Heaslip

Other two were up now so put on our trunks and staggered out for a bathe. Heavy mist all round, could hardly see pier on other side of the bay; grass very wet and a drizzle. Lovely bathe all the same. George and Michael did usual good dives off the pier. ...

We started off for the first time with waterproofs on, heading for Cleggan to work the north cliffs ... Kept up a good steady pace – everything looked very different in the mist which wreathed and twisted in phantom wraiths everywhere, making familiar objects and hilltops look strange and fantastic. Brockley farm, where I had a chat with McCurdy, then over the hills to Cleggan where I talked with Owen Murphy who told me that the barnacle

goose that he got winged in 1921 just died last year, so he had it for 27 years: some age for a goose![4]

Sun beginning to dispel the mist. Had a wonderful bathe in Cleggan lough, then pranced around in the short mountain grass to dry ourselves. George set up camera and took a photograph of us nude. The lake is in a beautiful setting, hills shutting it in on all sides – one hillside a resting place for hundreds of herring gulls, the grass burnt completely off with guano. From here we headed east along terrific cliffs – sheer in most places 400

---

4 Arnold first visited Rathlin in 1922. Over numerous subsequent visits he befriended many of the islanders and lighthouse-keepers, who often gave him a bed for the night (Loughie McQuaig still remembers him with affection). He returned their kindnesses by sending them parcels of books from the mainland.

feet. Could look straight down below you and see guillemots, razorbills and puffins swimming about in sea. As we approached the little tarn – so close to the cliff that it almost spills over the edge – where we saw the buzzard on Saturday, we were very cautious but not particularly hopeful. "Here's the place" said George, "look out boys." Michael and I scanned the tarn and the boggy patch around it, but nothing doing. Then swinging our eyes seawards George and I saw her. The buzzard was below us heading toward the corner of a cliff. With one frantic yell to Michael to run towards the edge, George and I stood trying to pick her up with binoculars. And when we succeeded we saw two birds, not one, but only a momentary glimpse then they were round the corner of the cliff eastwards. Great excitement! I dashed over to Michael and we gazed longingly in the direction they had disappeared. George joined us and now we enjoyed a lovely treat. Both buzzards and four ravens appeared in a great amphitheatre ahead of us and we had a great exhibition of soaring, the buzzards gracefully sweeping round in the updraught from the face of the cliff, the ravens angrily because they rightly considered this to be their territory – as they had nested here for nobody knows how long – while the large brown hawks are only interlopers. Occasionally a raven would stoop at a buzzard when the latter would yelp in a most undignified manner and swerve. One landed on prominent rock but the ravens put it off, then the other buzzard pitched in a rock chimney and stayed there until its mate and the ravens disappeared round the headland. Both birds showed marked interest in a particular section of cliff but I could see no nesting ledge. ... We found two buzzard's feathers on the clifftop, one of which I strongly suspect as being from a juvenile – let us hope so.

Three years later, after the Irish buzzards bred successfully for the first time.[5]

I was standing one bright day in May on the top of the north cliffs on Rathlin Island watching a buzzard slowly

Michael Benington, Buzzard on nest,
24 May 1956

circling four hundred feet above the sea, just opposite me, when with a yell "Kek, kek, kek, kek" out came a peregrine from its nest cliff – absolutely mad with rage – not straight at the buzzard, but rising steeply to get above it.

I watched fascinated. Then the falcon dived – a power dive: down, down, down she came, like a stone at the buzzard as if she would go clean through it. I fastened my glasses on the buzzard, and I can tell you it fastened its glance steadily on the peregrine. And at the psychological moment the buzzard rolled over, turned upside down, to present a set of eight sharp-hooked talons to the falcon. At this the peregrine side-slipped with amazing precision and skidded past it with only inches to spare. Now it looked as if nothing could check its headlong descent into the sea. But with frantically beating wings it just managed to recover itself at the bottom of the loop and climbed again just as steeply – breathtaking to watch.

In effect the peregrine swung on an eight hundred foot arc, swinging up with its own impetus almost as quickly as it dived. Then down again on the buzzard, only again to be deterred at the last second by the well-timed roll and the upturned claws. Of course split-second timing was required on both their parts. If they had struck I'm sure both birds would have been killed. A dangerous game to play. But real live drama! Most exciting to watch these

5 From BBC radio script 'What does Nature mean to you?' for National Nature Week, 19 May 1963, chaired by Peter Scott with contributions from Bert Axell, Tony Soper, Walter Flesher, Arnold Benington, Henry Douglas Home, Fred Lexster and Bill Condry.

two anything-but-good neighbours pursuing their age-old tactics of trying to discourage one another from nesting on the same cliff. Unfortunately a very rare sight now: we have so few falcons left.[6]

The Road to Nowhere; an account of a day in the Antrim Glens, from Winter Nature Diary 1947[7]

The rain is coming down in sheets, and a strong wind that is blowing doesn't seem to be able to make any break in the leaden grey sky. Just the kind of day to stay indoors with a nice bright fire. But there is no fire in my studio, yet I am well content. I have just had afternoon tea, not served by a white-capped maid, but out of a well worn rucksack pocket. My studio has a stone floor covered with springy turf and beautifully carved rock walls. There is a magnificent view, but no glass in the windows. Yet the rain is not beating in, nor is the wind annoying me.

As I came along this way an hour ago, the sunlight on the Glen was beautiful, but threatening clouds soon closed over and I climbed up into my cave. Here I really have a grandstand view, where I can sit on my perch and watch the wildlife unobserved. And it is wild! Untamed, and unspoiled. Presently, if the day clears up I shall 'Arise and go', though not to Innisfree, but for the same reason that the writer of that lovely poem courted solitude. I shall take the little road and follow it until it dwindles to a mere path and then dies out altogether. There, with the piping of sea birds and the music of the waves, I shall find peace.

Sitting here I am reminded of some lovely lines from the song that Moira O'Neill called "Lookin' Back", for

Rathlin Island lies across the stormy Waters o' Moyle, shrouded in mist and o'erhung by a pall of purple-black cloud against which fishing gannets stand out ghostly white. On the rocks below me a row of grotesque, fully fed cormorants stand like black gargoyles, with foam and spray at times almost covering them. At last it begins to clear and I climb down from my look-out.

How refreshing it is to … get away from the ugly straight lines of brick and mortar, from concrete footpaths and asphalt roadways, and forget the work-a-day world for a while. You may call this escapism: I call it re-creation. Since we give out energy all the time when we are working we must rebuild it somehow and store it. Well, this is my way of doing that … As I left my cave the little road wound and dipped so that at no time could I see for more than a couple of hundred yards ahead, and at each turn the scenery grew wilder. Finally the road became a cart track, and a poor one at that, and here stood the last cottage. From the cliff above there had been a fall of rock some time past and now a huge square slab of rock stood where it had come to rest just a few yards from the house. It appeared to menace the building, was almost a threat to the habitation of man. As if in obedience to this challenge, after this spot was passed I saw scarcely a trace of man: no road, no cars, no smoke of fire, no house, nothing man-made, no harrowing contrast of rich and poor. You meet none that look down on you and none that seek your favour. You may be lucky enough to meet an old fisherman or shepherd with whom you tarry a while and talk as an equal. I met one such, mahogany-tanned and clear-eyed, and we passed the time of day and discussed sheep for a while before I passed on. Now the path became a mere track, sometimes well marked, at others hard to find. At one spot it swung back like a miniature mountain road in a Swiss pass. Next, it was completely obliterated by a huge landslide. Large sandstone boulders blocked the way and a narrow passage like a staircase which just admitted my bulky rucksack had

---

6 Peregrines and Buzzards are now commonly seen around the Rathlin coastline. A regular boat service connects Ballycastle on the mainland with Church Bay on the island, whence a bus is available for those visiting the RSPB reserve at the West Lighthouse. With bed and breakfast accommodation also on offer, the primitive conditions Arnold experienced are long gone.

7 From Winter Nature Diary, unpublished manuscript, 1947, chapter 17

Michael Benington, Peregrine hunting rock dove, 2006 (detail)

to be found between two of these. Here, among the sandy soil from these fallen rocks, I found a grand colony of that scarce and beautiful flower, grass of parnassus, growing as profusely as daisies in a pasture. They looked rather like white buttercups, but the leaves are quite different. Instead of the divided leaf of the buttercup, this plant has small round leaves. ...

Surprisingly now the track broadened out to a level green sward, with a turf like velvet, and again it narrowed down to a hand-breadth with a steep rising bank on one side and a sudden drop on the other. All the way the herbage was beautiful. From the shingle of the beach below to the tops of the cliffs towering above, there was a real kaleidoscope of colours on the slopes. Bracken, scree and heather were interspersed with ragwort, scabious, bell heather, hare bells, lovely grasses and brightly coloured moss. It was a delight to the eye. Rounding a bluff now I came on a very overgrown stretch with tall bracken and brambles, jumbled rocks and big crags towering over all. Suddenly there was a movement ahead and a small flock of frightened sheep dashed up a steep incline and came to bay on a rock ledge, with horny heads turned outwards. I waited expectantly. Perhaps it was a fox! ...

Near the foot of a lovely waterfall was an unexpected piece of level sward on which one could have almost marked out a football pitch. In one corner of this was a heather patch, on which, to my delight I got a dozen large, velvet brown caterpillars of the fox moth. Overhead a family party of choughs dived and tumbled, throwing themselves about in the air as if the very joy of living were too much for them. Near the same spot, the short guttural croak of a raven carried two hundred yards against the wind to where I was standing, in spite of the ceaseless roar of the waves just below me. It was grand to see that those two uncommon crows were holding their own in this wild place. A sudden burst of sunshine now enriched everything in an almost startling manner. The leaden grey of the sea changed to an almost Mediterranean

Michael Benington, Raven nestling, 14 April 1956

hue, and the changing light on the crags above was a joy to see. Alas! It was only a momentary gleam. As suddenly as it had come the sun disappeared and rain began to fall. The dusk, too, began to drop down and I thought the time had come to turn homewards. Off the point, a late collier ploughed her way towards some distant port, against a strong tide-race. In spite of the failing light fulmar petrels, those peerless exponents of effortless gliding, were still on marine patrol. Curlews called, and I swung steadily homewards in the falling rain, well content with my lot. With such a changing scene to rest the eyes, and over this kind of ground, a man could walk fifteen to twenty miles without feeling more than pleasantly tired, whereas a mile over unyielding pavements is nearly enough for me.

Now a new note was heard, a small, yet strident and somehow urgent call. This was the alarm note of a wren and it came from somewhere on the scree slope above me. I flattened myself expectantly against a rock, for this tiny watchman rarely gives a false alarm. Almost immediately a large grey bird streaked like an arrow across the face of the cliff, checked suddenly opposite a ledge, then shot rapidly upwards for a hundred feet. It was the peregrine falcon hunting for its supper, and it had spotted a rock dove roosting on the ledge. The dove seemed to know that it was safe as long as it remained on the rock. The falcon, on the other hand was trying to frighten it off so that it could strike it down in the air. With this intention the peregrine dived down at full speed along the cliff face whizzing past the ledge as close as it dared, in an attempt to flush the rock pigeon. Then up she swung again at the end of her dive, with powerful beating wings, for another attempt. Three times she dived down past that crag, like a feather pendulum swinging in a six hundred foot arc. The impression of speed and power that she gave was astonishing. At the end of a dive she seemed to climb just as easily and as fast as she had come down. The rock dove wisely remained on the ledge. The proximity and dash of the bird of prey had not put her up, so the peregrine gave up in disgust and went off. Nevertheless she did not go to roost hungry, for I had not gone more than a hundred yards when I saw her again, flying along the top of the cliff with prey in her talons. She had been successful at last and, as I looked, she closed her wings and came down like a stone with the feathers of her prey trailing out behind her, like smoke from the exhaust of a fighter plane. Landing on a broad ledge, she began to pluck out the larger feathers of the bird before beginning to eat it, and at this stage I slipped away, anxious not to disturb her at such a well-earned meal.

The light had now grown much poorer and I had to watch my steps on the path, yet I kept constantly turning my head over my shoulder to watch the sky.

"Day declining, shed a softer gleam."

The saffron yellow in the west was a pleasant change after the overcast, leaden hue. It had been a grand day and I felt much refreshed. Perhaps you may wonder what all the excitement was about, just what I got out of it all? Well, unless you try it for yourself, it's rather difficult to explain. The pursuit of beauty for its own sake, this intimate contact with nature brings its own reward.

"In quietness and confidence shall be your strength."

As I paused for a minute for my last look back over the sea, a party of sea pies, piping shrilly, was silhouetted for a moment in echelon against the sunset. Two hours later, as I crept thankfully between the sheets, the oyster catchers were still calling "Good Night."

Tarka the otter, field diary entries 1950[8]

Tarka the otter arrived – a lovely beast. Cecil [Graham] brought her from a friend of his who found her on a river bank in early August. He wants a home for her in the country.

9.00 p.m. Jeannette and I brought Tarka into the house and enjoyed her company so much that we could hardly get to bed. Playful as a puppy and most affectionate. When at last we did put her out into the yard at night, she whistled and whined for company.

One week later: 10.00-10.45 p.m. Had Tarka into the house for a meal of herring, and a game. She was in great form – very affectionate, and appears to be boneless, the way she rolls and twists about on the floor and turns fantastic somersaults. She played for a long time with a banana skin growling and whining at it, then finally when I put her out to her quarters for the night, she whistled beautifully in the yard.

Three days later: Cicely and Kathleen [of the BBC] came out with Bill Tullough to make some recordings of Tarka, but though she behaved beautifully she remained dumb.

---

8 Nature Diary, unpublished manuscript, entries for 31 October, 7, 11 and 17 November 1950

Of course half an hour afterwards she whistled beautifully, whined and even barked once. From 9.00-10.00 p.m. alone with me in the sitting room she talked to me in a very attractive affectionate tone, sort of birdy notes. But she is very restless – would almost pull the upholstery to bits. Several times when running about over the floor she came to my feet and whined to be lifted. A most affectionate creature, and very gentle in that mood.

The next day: Tarka is about four months old now and measures 32 inches, including 12 inches tail. I put her in the swimming bath at school, to the great delight of numerous spectators. It was really marvellous to watch her swimming, with all four feet, both on the surface and underneath. Such speed and agility! She spent the whole day at school being played with and admired by all and sundry.

Six days later: I took Tarka in to the BBC today to have her photographed. She behaved splendidly but the photographer was not first class, and the results left much to be desired. After that Tarka went the round of the offices, much admired by all. She was on her best behaviour. About 5.45 Dr Chisholm arrived by car from Ballyclare where he now proceeded to take us both for my class in the High School. Again Tarka behaved perfectly, patiently allowing herself to be handled by everbody. After my class Dr Chisholm drove us back again to Belfast, where I most reluctantly handed our beloved Tarka over to [name omitted] who found her as a few days-old cub, apparently deserted.

James Lockhart, Arnold, Jennifer and friend with 'Tarka', 1950

Broadcasts

Michael Benington, Manx shearwaters at sea, 2005 (detail)

Stalking wild swans; 2 November 1925, retold for the BBC 1970[9]

At that time I lived out in the country about a mile from the River Lagan and had a small light canoe covered with fabric, like a miniature coracle. And when I wanted to move it from one point to another, that was done in the same way as the coracle – over the shoulder. In those days, as now, the river flooded periodically in winter, particularly at one place about a mile away where it ran through a flat marshy area.

One day ... during the floods, I was cycling along a muddy lane when I heard this electrifying sound – swans calling. "Wild swans," I said to myself, threw the bicycle down and got under the hedge. Here I raised my head carefully and peered through the bare twigs. A couple of hundred yards away the flooded river opened out into a kind of lake, thirty or forty acres in extent, and on this I could see a lot of wildfowl, amongst them over fifty wild swans. Focusing my binoculars as well as I could through the hedge, I thought the swans were whoopers, that is, the larger of the two wild species. The whooper is the Icelandic swan, the one that breeds on many of the lakes there in the summer and has less black on the tip of its beak than the bewick's swan from Siberia. I thought a lot of the duck were wigeon and many of the larger ones looked like mallard, with possibly some tiny teal among them. But I couldn't be certain of my identification because of the distance and the rather poor light. It was frustrating: there were the birds, here was I with my binoculars, and I could do nothing to bridge the gap between. If I'd got through a hole in the hedge and started to walk or crawl across the marsh towards the birds, they'd have got up and left in a body, or rather several different flocks.

So I turned sorrowfully homeward, but, as I rode through the puddles on that muddy track, I had an idea, a plan. Why not use my canoe? And that's what I did.

Next day I cut a lot of reeds and stuck them all around the gunwale. Actually, the canoe was already pretty well camouflaged because it was covered with a khaki-coloured fabric; but now with the fringe of reeds it was perfect. And as I set out I had high hopes. At first all went according to plan. I paddled easily downstream for a mile or so, and in another five minutes I'd have come in sight of my quarry – when I got the surprise of my life. Without any warning the canoe tipped over and I was thrown into the water. You'll get some idea of the expanse and depth of that flood when I explain that I'd been capsized by the top branches of a willow tree which of course was totally submerged.

When my head came above water, the canoe had floated away out of reach on the current. I took a quick look round. There was a hump-backed bridge about two hundred yards down-river. That would be a place to avoid. I didn't care for the idea of having my head bashed against the stonework by the swirling eddies of the river as it forced its way under the arches.

So I struck out as hard as I could at right angles to the current, and made for the road which ran parallel to the river, maybe a hundred and fifty yards away. As a family we had done a lot of swimming, with my father; so there wasn't really much to this. But I wasn't exactly dressed for swimming, and I was wearing thigh waders. These things are hard enough to get in and out of when one's on terra firma, so I didn't waste my time trying here. They were a bit heavy and clumsy and awkward to swim in, but not too bad. In fact, at the end they turned out almost to be a blessing in disguise; for when, after stemming the current and winning my race so to speak, I approached the road hedge, I touched down on top of a submerged blackthorn thicket. But it felt like the softest sand to me, and I struggled out onto the half-flooded road with a

---

9 From BBC radio script 'Country Window', introduced by Sam Hanna Bell, Radio Ulster, 25 October 1970

Arnold Benington, Michael and friend in the canoe that capsized, about 1938

terrific feeling of elation at first. I never wear a hat, or I expect I should have thrown it in the air. And I was a bit water-logged to jump with joy. But when I sobered down a bit and I remembered my belongings – my watch! Yes, still on my wrist, but probably not improved much by the immersion. And binoculars. My inflexible rule here of wearing them around my neck had stood me in good stead once more, and I hoped they could be cleaned and reset. But my sketchbook with all the season's drawings and notes – gone forever. A real loss. I was fortunate with the

canoe, however. It was washed ashore some miles further down, and I recovered it later.

When I had time to think about my experience, I was grateful to God for my escape, but I had no cause to thank my fellow man. Just before I was tipped overboard I remembered happening to notice two chaps leaning over the hump-backed bridge – perhaps enjoying the view. And, my word, they certainly had a grandstand view of my escapade. Being down-river of me, everything was coming their way, so to speak, and they just stood their

Michael Benington, Whooper swans over flooded fields, 2009

ground. They showed great calm. No flap, no fussing. Just let me get on with the job. They probably thought I was making a film or something.

And I believe they were still standing there as I squelched tiredly across the road and went off to look for my canoe.

The Story of Hush Wing, the long-eared owl; for the BBC 1948[10]

One dark night in the middle of May a large taxi was driving along a winding country road through a wood. As there was nobody about at this late hour, he was going fairly fast and, coming suddenly round a bend, nearly ran over a small grey object in the road. It looked at first like a kitten, but the driver was not satisfied and being a kind hearted man, he drew up the car and got out. To his great surprise it turned out to be a baby long-eared owl, or owlet, about ten days old. ... Although the driver

10 From Northern Ireland BBC radio script, 'Children's Hour', 26 May 1948, presented by Cicely Mathews. When full grown, the owl was successfully released into the wild.

approached with the best of intentions, the little bird tried to look fierce and hissed and snapped bravely. In spite of this however he was picked up as carefully as possible and placed in the boot of the car, which then drove off. ...

Just before midnight struck I was standing at the window in my pyjamas having a last look out. ... There was a glare of headlights dancing on the trees beside the road; the hum of an engine; the squeal of brakes – and a large black taxi stopped at my door. At first I thought it had come to the wrong house, but my gate squealed, then I heard the crunch of gravel and a bang at the front door.

Rather puzzled, I grabbed a dressing gown and hurried downstairs. Putting on the light I opened the door and there stood a figure in dark uniform; "Are you Mr. Benington?"

"Yes" I answered, and waited, wondering what was coming next.

"I found a young owl – at least I think that's what it is – on the road near Ballynahinch. It must have fallen out of a nest."

"And have you brought it?" I broke in eagerly.

"Aye! It's out here in the boot of the car. It would have died if I'd left it on the road and I thought maybe you could rear it." I thanked the man profusely and assured him that I would do my best to feed and care for it; as a matter of fact I was very glad of the chance, and it was kind of the taxi driver to come so far out of his way at that late hour. Then I turned my attention to the owlet. By this time he'd got thoroughly entangled in the folds of my dressing gown, so I carried him into the house as he was and put him in a large wooden box with plenty of straw bedding. But he wasn't the least grateful for all these attentions; in fact he strongly resented them, and when I put my face too close he hissed, spat and snapped his beak, in a truly ferocious manner. At least he meant it to be ferocious and would perhaps have succeeded if he hadn't been so ridiculously fluffy-looking and sleepy. And of course by this time I was fairly sleepy too, so covering him up carefully for the night I left him.

Next morning I said nothing to the children until … they were dressed. … Anyway they fairly rushed things that morning, and when they gathered round the box and I lifted the lid, I honestly don't know which was more surprised – the owlet or the children. There was one breathless moment when the children were actually speechless with amazement, then the flood burst forth and I could never begin to tell you all the things they said and asked me. Naturally they were delighted, and after the newcomer had got used to being stared at and talked to at a range of about two feet, he just sat and blinked and accepted the inevitable. Before long he had accepted and swallowed several small pieces of raw meat, and from that moment he was one of the family. They fed him so satisfactorily that when I came home at lunch the owlet – having eaten all the food that would normally have been shared with three or four brothers and sisters – was absolutely, well, you know the way you feel after a party! I think Jennifer must have been at home that morning as well as Fiona, for on the box was printed, in rather crooked letters "SHUTEYE". I was amused at this for the name was most appropriate, especially when he was well fed. He would shut one eye and leer at you with the other in a half bemused and wholly comical fashion.

For the first week or so we kept his box in the kitchen where my long suffering wife kept an eye on him – and Fiona during my absence. At first the children didn't know whether to call him Shuteye or Fluffy and so far as appearance was concerned there wasn't much to choose between them, for he was delightfully soft.

It was at this stage that I first introduced him to Cicely [Matthews, the presenter]. Going in to Broadcasting House one day to give a talk, I took him with me and managed to get into the studio before Cicely. Then opening his box I lifted him out and perched him on the edge, where he sat blinking and looking most attractive just as she walked in. …

But by this time feeding him was no joke. Meat of any kind was so scarce [rationing was still in force] that we

Michael Benington, Young long-eared owl nestling, 1947

couldn't depend on a daily supply so we sent out a special SOS to farmers and others in the district to keep us any mice they got; as a matter of fact I put an advertisement in the local paper, and people were very good about it. There was a fairly steady stream of mice, rats, dead birds of all kinds and cat's meat, and in return for their trouble in bringing the scraps we usually invited the donors to come into the shed and watch our pet being fed. Of course Hushwing didn't mind any number of spectators – he was used to them by this time – so long as they kept fairly quiet and let him get on with the important job of eating. It was great fun to watch him, and although he was usually ravenous and gulped his food down whole, you couldn't help noticing his gentleness. Like well brought up boys and girls he didn't grab or snatch, but took the mouse or whatever it was gently, and in a couple of vigorous gulps swallowed it head first. By this time he would fly and came when called to an outstretched hand, without any swishing of wings. His silence in flight was marvellous and of course led to the name of Hushwing. ... It was difficult to get used to his sudden appearance, without any accompanying noise. He would suddenly plop down on your shoulder or head without any warning. It was rather an eerie experience in a way. But nearly everything about Hushwing was different – I think that was the secret of his popularity – he wasn't a bit like other birds, except that he had feathers. You know I can't understand how anyone can shoot an owl – they're so fascinating to watch – let alone their usefulness.

Cicely (laughing): I'll never forget the second time you brought him in to see us, when he was grown up, at least a lot more grown up than the first time.

Arnold: You know there was very little work done in Broadcasting House that day, the staff followed him in a crowd wherever he went, but he was a prime favourite of yours Cicely, what did you find so attractive about him?

Cicely: Oh, everything! His bright yellow eyes, and that funny habit he had of wobbling his head from side to side and up and down.

Arnold: Yes! Of course all owls do that. ... But I think that habit was particularly amusing when he was approached at close range by one of the photographers that day in Broadcasting House. He wanted a real close up and the camera was poked almost in Hushwing's face. He wasn't scared, but was he interested? My word – he stared at it this way and that up and down, twisted his head round and swung it about until we thought he would tie his neck in knots, then suddenly he lost interest in it and flew up on to the microphone where he perched of his own free will, and looked back over his shoulder at the delighted photographer, as much as to say "Now, is that the pose that you want?"

Cicely: Yes ... and didn't we make some more recordings of him too?

Arnold: We did indeed, Frank made several and when he had finished I took Hushwing into the studio on my wrist and Frank played over one of the discs. It was the funniest thing to see his reactions to his own voice. He listened to me talking, then his reply – all coming from a sort of black-box in the corner – then he turned round and looked at the real me and was completely puzzled.

Northern Ireland's first bird observatory; for the BBC 1954[11]

There were already a dozen bird observatories round the British coast before we got one in Ireland at all. Then three or four years ago Major Ruttledge founded one on the Great Saltee Island. I believe it's a real success – they get all kinds of migrants, but it is off Wexford, rather too far away to be much use to Ulster birdwatchers, so we began to cast round for something more suitable. Away back in 1936 or '37, one summer when I was staying for holidays in Dundrum Bay, there was some very wet stormy weather. I got into the habit of going to St. John's Point where a long narrow promontory juts out eastward into the Irish Sea, to watch for seabird movement. And I was interested to find that it was a good observation point especially with regard to manx shearwaters. From that point I regularly saw them passing, mostly northwards, with the graceful, effortless, undulating flight that is so characteristic. Some days thousands passed – I sat and counted them on the hard, hard rocks – and to this day I haven't got a really satisfactory explanation for the huge numbers. But it dawned on me that there must be a breeding colony somewhere in County Down (at that time

---

11 From BBC radio script, 'A New Bird Observatory', Northern Ireland Home Service, 27 September 1954 (the year the observatory was established on Old Lighthouse Island).

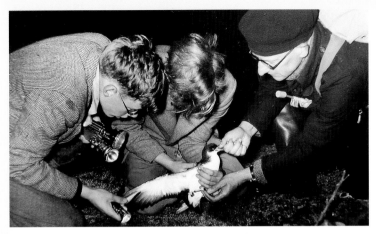

Unknown photographer, Arnold Benington with
two boys ringing manx shearwaters, Copelands

Michael Benington, Copeland Bird Observatory, 1954

the only one known in Northern Ireland was on Rathlin).
Shortly afterwards I told Mr Douglas Deane of my theory,
and next year, 1939, he and my late friend Denis Rankin
found a shearwater sitting on an egg in a burrow on
Lighthouse Island – the first breeding record for County
Down.

In 1941 four ornithologists spent a couple of nights on
the island – that's the middle one of the Copeland group:
the one that's now the observatory. ... In the short time
that they had they made quite a comprehensive study of
the birds on both outer islands, especially perhaps the
terns – and that account makes very interesting reading
now, for comparison with our findings of the last couple
of years.

In 1947 I stayed there a couple of nights myself, and
saw the possibilities of the place as a spot for observing
birds, but at that time the idea of a bird observatory
hadn't occurred to me.[12] It was three years later, in 1951,
that various ornithological bodies began making enquiries
about some islands and promontories, with the idea of ...
establishing some sort of a bird observatory. ... In one

way the Copelands seemed an obvious choice. It was
conveniently placed for many birdwatchers in Northern
Ireland, but was it good for migrating birds? ...

The Ulster Society for the Protection of Birds ...
arranged a rota of observers to visit Lighthouse Island
every weekend during the migrating season. And in fact a
good many visits were paid by people who gave up the
time and spent a couple of nights roughing it in the ruins
of the old lighthouse. Unfortunately, however, nearly all
the results were negative: and after a while interest in the
idea died down a lot because, well – after all you must
have plenty of birds for a bird observatory and there just
seemed to be no migrants on the Copelands, or next to
none anyway ...

On Lighthouse Island, we have been studying birds by
day and catching shearwaters by night with the aid of good
bright torches. We usually get three or four hours sleep
towards the morning, just lying on the floor of the old
ruins, on beds of bracken, and cooking on a driftwood
fire; one night last summer as we lay there, just before
dropping off to sleep one of the men said – "Wouldn't it
be a good idea to buy this island, then we could come any
time we liked to study birds?" And that remark was the
germ of the idea. Of course none of us had all that money

12 In August 1947 Arnold took a BBC recording crew with him to
Lighthouse Island to capture the sounds of the Shearwaters calling in
their burrows. The results featured in a broadcast, 'Shearwater Island',
aired on the Northern Ireland Home Service on 20 October 1947.

Michael Benington, Head of manx shearwater ringed on Copelands

to spare, but we did club together to lease the island, and I must say that we've found our landlord to be most generous and helpful. In fact without his wholehearted co-operation the scheme would not have been possible. Of course it is only in its infancy yet, but it's a lusty growing child, and is already providing useful recreation for a lot of men and women, who go out when they can and divide their time between studying birds and doing necessary repair jobs to the buildings. Most of these are just shells, but some of them require very little more than a roof to make them habitable. ...

Our island covers forty acres of rough ground, rising about ninety feet to a mound on which the ruins stand. The shore is rocky with three possible landing places, and sixty-foot cliffs running along the east side. A well, just above high water mark provides us with an apparently inexhaustible supply of good water, which of course has to be carried up to the house.

So far we have seen seventy-eight species of birds from time to time on the island, and no doubt we shall extend that number considerably before long, but our chief reason for existing is, of course, the study of the breeding population. In that category we have about 900 hundred

pairs of herring gulls, about 50 pairs of lesser black-back gulls, 15 to 20 pairs of greater black-backs, a few common gulls and a few black-headed, about 200 pairs of common and arctic terns and a few roseates, about 200 pairs of shearwaters – of which we succeeded in catching and ringing 270 individuals; half a dozen pairs of stock doves nesting in rabbit burrows, 6 pairs of jackdaws, 4 species of nesting ducks – mallard, eider, shelduck and merganser – , about 10 pairs of moorhen and a lot of smaller birds: swallows which nest in the hostel, rock pipits, sedge warblers, linnets, hedge sparrows, wrens and so on. As well as these we have occasional exciting visitors like greylag goose, peregrine falcon, merlin, short-eared owl, storm petrel, great northern and red-throated divers, and probably a lot more if we were able to be there more frequently.

Nowadays most people will have heard or read about the British Museum scheme for marking individual birds with a numbered aluminium ring on the leg. When many birds have been ringed, caught again and released and so on we eventually learn the maximum age of the species

Unknown photographer, Arnold Benington and unknown boy in front of Lighthouse Island, Copelands

– also the average age, and something about its migration movements. This of course is a slow business – a real long term policy but it does inevitably yield results – and is undoubtedly fascinating. But it's not the only thing we do. We weigh and measure specimens caught, to find out causes for fluctuation in weight, examine them for parasites; keep a count of the various populations; study the hatching and fledging; make lists of the island's insects and plants, and so forth.

In a nutshell I should say our aim is to get an overall picture of the relationships that exist between the many forms of life that are found there – not always in harmony, but certainly dependent upon one another in some way if we could only find it. We don't aim to keep this island exclusively to ourselves. Indeed we would like to see the island become a sort of open air extra mural training college in ornithology.

Journey to Iceland, In the Lava Desert; for the BBC 1955[13]

We arrived in Reykjavik on June 2, and spent nearly a week in the south at Thingvellir, near the site of the ancient 1000 year old Parliament or Althing. Of course there are no railways in Iceland – transport is by bus, jeep, truck or pony. There are roads of a sort round the coast, and these connect up the farms and scattered villages where sheep farming and fishing are about the only industries. In the interior there are only ice caps, marshes and black lava deserts, and few people penetrate …

---

13 From BBC radio script, Northern Ireland Home Service, 12 August 1955. The expedition, which lasted from 28 May to 6 July 1955 (including nine days out and back), necessitated a great deal of preparation, including transporting enough dry foods to sustain the whole team while camping for a month. The other team members were Michael Benington, Jack Gray, Gordon Greeves, Herbert Jeffery, Jack (Dusty) Miller, Brian Moller and John Wilson.

When we took the coastal bus to the north we heard that the road had been washed away by mountain torrents, owing to the melting of snow fields during the good weather, and it would be several days before the road would be usable again. However, our time was very valuable, and rather than wait in the south we hired a four-wheel drive truck, which we were told would take us anywhere, through anything: and it did too! It cost us £50 to drive from Reykjavik, the capital in the south, the odd 300 miles to beautiful Akureyri on a northern fjord, but it was well worth it in the saving of time.

On the way we drove through the most lovely scenery imaginable, up one side of a fjord and down the other, through ragged mountain passes, over high wild moorland with snow on either side of us, round innumerable hairpin bends where one slip would have been just too bad, and finally through two rivers which were in such spate that they had carried away their bridges, and threatened at any moment to do the same to us and our truck, gear, food and all. In the middle of that torrent with the water boiling up round the radiator and coming through the floor, and the rumble of boulders as they were swept down, there was as much excitement as we wanted for

Arnold Benington, On board the MV Gullfoss en route to Iceland, 1955. Left to right: Brian Moller, Gordon Greeves, Jack Gray, Michael Benington, Dusty Miller and Herbert Jeffery

Unknown photographer, Arnold Benington
emerging from hide, Iceland, 1955

everywhere and the high degree of respect with which
they treated other people's property. ...

Lake Myvatn where we had been staying is a really
wonderful place for birds. We were very happy there
studying at close quarters twelve of the fourteen species of
wild duck, slavonian grebes, short-eared owls, snow
buntings, Greenland wheatears, mealy redpolls, ptarmigan,
white wagtails, arctic skua and many other different kinds
of birds; so you might be excused for wondering why we
should willingly leave for the barren lava of central
Iceland.

The answer put very briefly is: because of the call of the
wild goose. We particularly wanted to see the pinkfeet
nesting and the Iceland falcon if possible; and both these
birds are shy and timid and found only on remote cliffs.
...

Very little was known regarding their [the pink-footed
goose's] breeding habits until about 65 years ago, when an
Icelandic farmer in search of some sheep followed the
course of the Skjalfandofljot river far into the interior.
There he saw some grey geese nesting on a cliff beside the
river ... From that time until 1920 the nesting pinkfeet in
that river gorge increased, up to about a thousand pairs,
then they decreased again just as steadily and just as
mysteriously. Several ornithological explorers have been to
Iceland during this century to solve the mystery of the
fluctuating numbers. ... David Haig Thomas ... was
inclined to think that the breeding birds periodically got
tired and moved their quarters. Recent work of Peter
Scott and others largely supports this view and made me
all the more anxious to fulfil a fifteen-year old ambition
and go to see for myself. The very large breeding colony
that Peter Scott discovered is in the south centre of
Iceland, but I wanted to go in from the north to Haig
Thomas's country. So on June 14, a bitterly cold morning,
four of us struck camp. It was snowing a little, which
didn't help, but by 8.30 we were all packed into a lorry
and off. Forty miles further on at Godafoss, a great

the moment – and we were very relieved when the truck
climbed safely out on the far side. ...

About the middle of the month we set off for central
Iceland, but before I describe the bird news of the interior
I want to tell you something about the people. Points that
particularly struck us were the national costume with
pigtails worn mostly by the older women; the friendly
children with their gaily coloured jeans, jerseys and
dungarees; the sturdy, independent, but kindly nature of
the farmers: the hospitality that we experienced

Arnold Benington, Pink-footed geese, Iceland, 1955

fast flowing Skjalfandofljot, but we enjoyed it a lot more when at 1.00 pm a pair of grey geese rose and flew up the river past us.

These were our first pinkfeet, and we noted the higher pitched voice and the more uniform grey plumage than the greylag. Now we were on tenterhooks to know if the geese were nesting in the area – until an hour later our guide suddenly pointed out a goose sitting on its nest on a cliff across the river. This was good news, but as the nest was inaccessible, we plodded on – through rocky gorges, desert sand and rough black lava until at last we reached the craggy valley that was our destination. Here our guide drew his pony to a stop and indicated that we had arrived. But before anybody had even dismounted I suddenly spotted a pink-footed goose sitting on its nest on top of a rock within twenty-five yards of us. I pointed it out wildly to the others – the goose flew off and we rushed excitedly over to see the nest – four large white eggs in a warm nest of grey down. Before we had time to realize our good fortune we heard a loud menacing cry and saw a large Iceland falcon circling overhead.

waterfall where the pagans are supposed to have thrown their idols at the coming of Christianity, we changed ourselves and gear to a jeep and trailer.

For nearly thirty miles now we bumped southwards over a rough track and through shallow rivers, always keeping to the course of the Skjalfandofljot river until in the early afternoon we reached our hill farm. As I had written to the farmer several times he was expecting us, but he … replied "Nay nestur au morgen" – indicating that the ponies would not be ready for us until tomorrow.

To save us unpacking everything we spent that night in an outhouse, comfortably bedded in hay, and were off next day on the ponies by eleven o'clock. Eight ponies there were altogether, including three pack – most carefully and skilfully loaded by the farmers – so much so indeed that not once during three or four hours riding over very rough and rocky country did our guide have to stop to readjust a load. We enjoyed that ride over the wild uninhabited country and alongside the gorge of he

Arnold Benington, Gyr falcon and young, Iceland, 1955

Arnold Benington, Truck loaded with gear, Iceland, 1955

This probably meant a nest, so we scattered quickly along the cliff to find it. Inside half an hour the guide had found it. I heard a shout and from the cliff edge where I was standing I saw the falcon pressing home a very determined attack. I hurried along and as Moller and I climbed up to the nest we also came under fire from the falcon. There were three hefty downy youngsters in the eyrie and as we handled these the falcon was frantic. She did not actually strike us but at least once she struck the rock just above my head, and altogether it was too convincing to be comfortable. ...

We built hiding places at both the falcon's and the goose nest — very carefully and very gradually so as not to frighten these rare and wary birds: then I hid inside to photograph them. ... The times I spent in those hides — sometimes fourteen hours at a time — were some of the most wonderful days in my life. After the patient labour of my three friends carrying large blocks of lava and building the hiding place, working like mad for a short spell every day for fear of scaring the geese, at last the goose flew unconcernedly on to the nest and, within twelve feet of me and my camera, pushed back the down off her eggs and calmly sat down to brood them. Then indeed was my cup of joy full. Another day, when after waiting eight hours in the falcon hide on such a narrow ledge that my only possible change in position was to stand gingerly up or sit gingerly down again on a tiny stool with my back against the cliff, I was beginning to think that the falcons had not succeeded in catching the usual ptarmigan for supper and were not going to come to the nest that day. Then at last I was startled by a loud thump and saw the huge fierce grey falcon standing on the ledge in front of me. That was the peak of achievement. And when, after glaring for five minutes at the hide it decided that all was well and walked forward to feed the young, there followed ten minutes of feverish excitement and activity on my part: pressing the shutter, rolling on the film, firing shot after shot as quickly and quietly as I could before the meal was over and the falcon took herself off again to stand guard on the cliff opposite.

One of my most vivid recollections is the day of the storm. I had been five hours in the hide waiting during lovely weather which would have been perfect for photography, then suddenly (as occasionally happens in Iceland) it darkened over and began to rain and blow. The hide rocked perilously, and I crouched against the rock wall almost afraid to move on my narrow ledge, but … although I got wet and rain also came in on the camera, neither of us was any the worse. The falcon came again and I got some quite good photographs: so all was well. And without going into any more details I'm glad to be able to say that the falcons were thriving and the geese eggs hatching as we reluctantly came away and the expedition ended on this happy note.[14]

Arnold Benington, Camp in the lava desert, Iceland, 1955

---

14 When Arnold arrived back with his family in Lisburn he had lost two stone in weight and, due to acclimatization to the midnight sun, he could not bear to go to bed. Nothing daunted, in July 1961 he returned to Iceland with eleven members of the ornithology class of the Belfast Workers Educational Association.

Articles

Unknown photographer, Arnold Benington with sparrowhawk nestling, 1964

Robins nesting in Ulster classroom; newspaper article 1966[15]

At the beginning of last week when the schools were reassembling after the holidays some boys came running up to me just before morning roll call to say that there was a robin's nest in their classroom.

"Yes," I said rather sceptically. "I'm sure!"

"Really sir, with four eggs," they replied.

I hurried on to my own collect wondering what kind of a stunt this was.

A few minutes later one of our men came to ask if he was to mend the broken window in a particular classroom.

"Why not?" I asked. "Well, if I mended it what will the robin do?" he replied.

So to save further discussion I went with him to see for myself. Just behind the door of the room is a row of lockers in which pupils keep books, and when I went in there were perhaps twenty boys and girls standing at these lockers excitedly discussing their find, and pointing out the nest to me. Sure enough there it was cosily tucked into an open locker on top of and among the books of 14-year-old Eric Erwin.

Later on in the morning I went back to the room and asked the mistress in charge if the robin had gone.

"Oh no," was the surprising answer. "We have left an opening in the broken pane for her beside my desk. She flies in and out there, perches on the radiator, then flies over the heads of the pupils to the nest. She seems to feel quite at home – and when the classes change at the end of the lesson she does not seem to mind the noise."

You could have knocked me down with a feather – a robin's feather!

Next day we had to do something about Eric's books, so I got him a lot of old text books and as opportunity offered he replaced essential ones with obsolete models. And still the bird sat on. Even while standing looking at the robin sitting there I can hardly believe it. So far the locker owner has manfully resisted the temptation to plead this unique excuse for homework not done – "Please, sir, there's a robin's nest on my French prep."

I think that this particular form feels that while many societies and clubs are running films, lectures, tours and exhibitions for National Nature Week we, too, are doing our stint. Not many children can boast that they reared young robins in their classroom!

Update, 12 May 1966: … our young classroom robins are coming on well. If we suspect that, through unintentional disturbance during schoolhours, the amount of food brought by the parents is insufficient, we supplement this by a supply of small worms. To our surprise and delight the female will take these out of the hand. But we control the amount of this artificial feeding very carefully.

The corncrake orphans who will fly; newspaper article 1967[16]

At this time of year one of the favourite topics of conversation is an exchange of views on how the summer holidays were spent. Many and varied are the answers given to the leading question here … But different from all these was the manner in which Ivan Topping occupied

---

15 *Belfast Newsletter*, 28 April and 12 May 1966

16 *Belfast Newsletter*, 8 September 1967. Forty years earlier, the first thing Arnold noticed upon returning from a year in England was the sound of Corncrakes everywhere. Sadly today the prevalence of factory farming means that there are no Corncrakes left in Ireland.

Arnold Benington, Corncrake at nest

himself. He worked for a good part of time on his uncle's farm in the direction of Stoneyford.

Early in June they were cutting a field of hay, and when they were coming near the middle with only a rood or two left standing, as was the custom he walked in front of the mower to flush any corncrakes, pheasants or rabbits so that they would not get cut to pieces as the reaper felled the last swathe. By this simple and humane method he saved the lives of many corncrakes and pheasants, and not a few hares as well.

One day shortly before "The Twelfth", while employing these tactics, he put out five or six corncrakes, and the knives passed over a nest with six eggs. When Ivan lifted these he could see they were hard set and thought it was an awful pity that all the young corncrakes should die in their shells. He knew of course that the parents, having had such a fright, would never return to eggs left without any cover in the middle of the cut field. So this is what he did – and he had to be quick about it before the eggs got

chilled. He collected them and wrapped them gently in a piece of cloth which he then put in a box on top of a stove to keep warm. Of course here it was impossible to regulate the temperature to the necessary 99 degrees Fahrenheit, but it was the best he could do for the moment.

Then suddenly he remembered a tame pigeon of his that had been sitting on eggs for about a week, so he removed the pigeon's two eggs and replaced them with six corncrake eggs. Surprised as it may have felt at this sudden increase in its maternal responsibilities the pigeon simply puffed out its feathers a bit more and managed to keep six eggs warm until next morning. Still Ivan was not satisfied that he had got the best possible foster mother, so he relieved the patient pigeon and put the corncrake's eggs under a bantam hen that was broody. Very soon all six eggs hatched and the bantam took great care of her tiny black, very active chicks.

Through circumstances over which the foster mother had no control four of the chicks died or came to grief, but by dint of much care and hard work digging for worms, slugs, slaters, earwigs and beetles, Ivan and the bantam between them have reared two of the orphan corncrakes through, almost, to flying stage. They are due any day now to be sent out into the big world all on their own – a great achievement by the boy who strove so hard for six weeks to bring about this great event.

Michael Benington, Corncrake

Unknown photographer, Arnold Benington,
top of Grey Man's Path, Fair Head

The return of the golden eagle to Ireland; magazine article 1955[17]

Looking back over the last couple of years I often think it would have been appropriate to have July 22nd marked red in all 1953 calendars, for that was the date on which I saw my first golden eagle's nest, and it was in Ireland, too, which made it all the more remarkable. It was the first 20th century golden eagle's nest in Ulster, and it had been found by a friend of mine [Gordon Greeves] a few days before.

It would not be true to say that he found the nest accidentally, but certainly it was without a great deal of preparation. It happened like this. For several weeks he had been working very hard, then one fine day he felt the need for a change and went off up the Antrim coast for a run in the car.

Eventually stopping the car at one of the many vantage points on this wonderful road, my friend got out to admire the view. And as he turned away from the car there was the eagle gliding high over the cliff top! At first he took it to be a buzzard, but even that was a rarity at that time, and he watched it carefully.

It was some distance off and probably did not see him, for in a few minutes it suddenly half closed its huge wings and dived straight down onto the cliff face. Thinking that this looked suspicious my friend set out to investigate, and after a long and tiring scramble reached a rocky vantage point near the spot where the eagle had dived. Here he sat and eagerly scanned the cliff below, and it was not long before the huge nest was spotted containing two large young birds-of-prey of some kind. They looked too large for buzzards, but my friend hardly dared hope that they might be golden eagles.

That night he rang up and we discussed the exciting possibility: "Eagles in Ireland! Couldn't be true!" Needless to say we arranged a date at the earliest possible minute. Actually it was three days later that we managed to get away (and these days felt like weeks), but we made up for it when we did get there. From a bird-watching point of view I suppose that was the greatest day of my life – and the greatest moment came when I perched carefully on a rock ledge, made sure of my footholds, and looked over. Just before my gaze shot downwards I noticed the smile on my friend's face. It lit up as he said "There you are now. I can do nothing more for you. Take your fill!" And I did. As my eyes slid downwards questingly I shall never forget the sort of shock as they came to rest on the nest and young. I felt immediately that they were eagles, and it is a wonder that I did not fall off the ledge in my excitement. Superlatives fail to convey the tremendous thrill

Michael Benington, Young golden eagle after first flight, 19 July 1958

17 'Days with the Golden Eagle,' Ulster Illustrated, Vol.3, No.1, February-March 1955, pages 34-35. A pair of eagles bred at Fair Head between 1953 and 1960, but not since. More recently, Golden Eagles have been re-introduced to Glenveagh National Park, Donegal.

Michael Benington, *Juvenile golden eagle hunting hare*

and excitement that were ours as we sat and gazed at the young in wonder and admiration ... "Where had the parents come from? How long had they been there?" were just two of the many questions that occurred to us. Perhaps my feelings at the time are best expressed by a note written in my pocket diary on the ledge.

"July 22nd – 1.30 p.m. Gazing down in rapture on eagle's nest. Marvellous sight. Two eaglets about full grown. Flapping wings several times standing on edge of nest, and showing white tail base well. Feet, beak and legs very yellow. Legs feathered to the toes – therefore can't be buzzards.

"2.30 p.m. Female eagle sailed round corner of cliff about 50 feet directly below me, and at same time male also appeared further off. What a sight! Four eagles in view at one time! Lazy flaps – huge wing span, etc., etc."

I heaved a sigh of pure bliss and with difficulty removed my gaze from the nest and let it roam far out over the sea. Then I stood up and looked slowly round at the mountains, moors and glens. It was all familiar country to me, yet somehow today it was different. It had taken on a new significance. Now it was "eagle country" ...

Although we stayed as long as we could that day watching the eagles and their young, we had to leave finally to return to so-called civilization, but I have been back many times since and have never yet drawn a blank. … There was the dull misty day when we saw her gliding over a hill tarn and gazing enquiringly down at a visiting whooper swan from Iceland. The eagle was hungry, but the whooper was a bit too big for her – and she sailed majestically on. One of the days was actually fine, and as we lay in the heather the pair of birds passed back and forwards over us several times.

Another time the male and female treated us to a tight formation exhibition. They flew so close together that for long minutes at a time both were viewed through one glass, and at times almost seemed to touch one another. On the wettest day of all, however, we got our very best view. The weather was so bad that I almost called it off, but I have a rooted objection to turning back, and we climbed as near as possible to the nest without a rope. Standing on a broad ledge below I was watching the young, delighted that the parents had succeeded in rearing a family again this year, when Michael who was close by said "Careful, Dad – look behind you." I turned my head slowly and there sure enough on a large rock about a hundred yards distant was, not one eagle – but two. Up till that we had never even seen one eagle perched; this wonderful sight was almost too much for me, and their subsequent behaviour almost more so. They sat there quite calmly as if their arch-enemy, man, was not within miles, then took off in turn and proceeded to fly, not away out over the sea, but towards us and the nest, and on slowly round the corner of the cliff. The most wonderful, and apparently staged, fly-past; obviously for our special benefit.

The decline of the sparrowhawk in Northern Ireland; journal article 1971[18]

Some fifty years ago, when, as a 16-year old schoolboy, I found my first sparrowhawk's nest, these birds were common in north Ireland. Up to about 1956, when the numbers were still high many pairs nested in very obvious places, usually successfully. For instance, one nested in an apple tree in an overgrown orchard, while another was in a hedgerow hawthorn with no woodland nearby.

In the early 1920s near Moira, I used to be able to go out early in the morning on my bicycle and visit two or three sparrowhawks' nests before breakfast. In half a day, in May or June, using the same transport, I could usually visit as many as six nests before dark. At that time inside a measured seven square miles of country around my home, there nested regularly eight pairs of sparrowhawks, five kestrels, five barn owls and three or four long-eared owls.

Since those days, however, a sad change has come over the numbers of birds of prey, although I do not think the owls have been quite so badly hit as others. Sparrowhawks have undoubtedly suffered most. From being a common species, quite suddenly they began to disappear. Territory after territory that I had known to be occupied consecutively for 30 or even 35 years, now fell empty; and during my country walks, instead of seeing a hunting hawk every few days, I no longer saw one even every two or three months.

Michael Benington, Young sparrowhawk, 6 July 1962

18 'The Decline of the Sparrow Hawk, Accipiter Nisus, in Northern Ireland', Irish Naturalists' Journal, Vol. 17 no.3, July 1971

I set out in 1959 to examine as many of the old-established territories as possible. I tackled the problem by taking a study area of some fourteen miles diameter, or approximately 160 square miles – in the midst of which I live and work. This is a sparsely wooded area with some rich arable land in the centre, a lot of good grazing, the town of Lisburn with some 18,000 inhabitants, several villages, and a fair amount of fenland on its west side, along the shore of Lough Neagh.

In this area 22 pairs of sparrowhawks nested regularly well within eight miles of my home, as a focal point.

In the period 1956 to 1966 the number of pairs of sparrowhawks had declined to six, a decrease of 73 per cent. I examined all the nests several times in a season and by observing the number of young to fledge from each clutch of eggs, I noted a serious drop in fertility as well.

Michael Benington, Female sparrowhawk on nest, 2006 (detail)

There is a fairly regular pattern of behaviour in one or two territories that I have been able to watch closely. For example, in a small wood near Lurgan, Co. Armagh (within the study area) from my notes:

1964   Five young were reared
1965   Three infertile eggs with pesticides present: two young reared
1966   No birds present
1967   No birds present
1968   Out of five eggs laid, two were infertile with pesticides present, one chick died, two young were reared
1969   Birds disappeared – site empty
1970   Birds disappeared – site empty

That this state of affairs is largely due to organochlorides absorbed into the hawks' tissues from horticultural and agricultural pesticides is strongly suggested by the analyses of infertile eggs that Dr Ian Presst kindly agreed to investigate for me at the Monks Wood Experimental Station, Huntingdon. Most eggs contained four of the following persistent organochlorine residues – dieldrin, DDT, TDE, heptachlore-poxide and DDE; with the last named always present in greatest quantity. …

Though I have some evidence that sparrowhawks are still being illegally destroyed from time to time, mainly in pheasant-rearing estates, this is nothing like as common as, say twenty years ago, when every farmer, gamekeeper, and skin collector shot them on sight: though in one way now it is more serious as the total population is so small.

It seems clear then that the decline is not due primarily to shooting, but rather to chemicals which showed up in every infertile egg that I sent for analysis in 1965 and 1968.

Unknown photographer, Arnold Benington at sparrowhawk nest

July 21. 1921.

The ground underneath Chestnut-trees is littered with small Chestnuts which have dried up and fallen off for want of rain.

July 25. 1921.

Jackdaw, Starlings & Rooks have banded together and are searching the fields for food in big flocks.

August 10. 1921.

Robins are singing again already.

One would think Autumn had come already to hear the Robin singing so sweetly these still, quiet days. Starlings also are singing again.

August 17 1921.

Swifts have left us now.

August 28. 1921.

Willow warblers have not gone yet.

Aug. 31. 1921.

Lime Trees have begun to shed their leaves.

Sept. 1. 1921.

Virginian creeper is beginning to colour a bit. Robins have begun their Autumn moult.

Sept. 4. 1921.

Sycamore leaves are showing reddish tints already.

Arnold Benington, Sparrowhawk, diary pages, 1921

It is interesting to compare over the years the population and breeding success levels. Allowing for errors and fluctuations due to unknown causes, once the decline really began, around 1957, it went down surprisingly quickly in 1967 to the frighteningly low level of 18 per cent of the pre-decline population.

Afterword by Jonathan Benington

As a boy growing up in Coleraine in the 1960s, I can remember Saturday morning shopping excursions when I would bump into schoolmates accompanied by their parents. On hearing my surname, the grown-ups would invariably ask if I was any relation of Arnold Benington, at which I would recoil in surprise for I was woefully ignorant of my grandfather's far-reaching influence as a pioneering nature writer and broadcaster. In truth I was too young to have heard his regular contributions to BBC Children's Hour, which went off the air in 1964, a victim of the newfound dominance of television over radio. I must also admit to having been intent, even then, on breaking the mould that had stood good for at least three generations of Beningtons, for my grandfather's prowess as a naturalist encompassed botany, at which his father Charles excelled, as well as the making of photographic and painted studies of wildlife, a skill he passed on to his son Michael.

It was only in 2002, twenty years after Arnold's death, that I began to appreciate the full extent of his legacy. This took the form of twenty-eight neatly written and illustrated volumes of field diaries, a box of hand-coloured lantern slides, several hundred articles for the Belfast Newsletter, and at least as many radio scripts preserved in the BBC Written Archive (sadly most of the sound recordings do not survive). Sifting through these and transcribing some 260,000 of his words started out as a family history exercise, but as the work progressed, the possibility of publishing some of them slowly dawned on me. Accompanied by sketches and photos, they would surely form what Philip Doughty of the Ulster Museum adjudged a "warm and sensitive record of landscapes now, sadly, no more and consequently all the more valuable for that."[19]

On seeing Arnold's words jump off the page at me after all that time, I was struck by their refreshing lack of jargon. Even for a reluctant birder such as myself, the spontaneity of his story-telling was infectious, fuelled as it was by a passion for his subject that impelled him to develop a uniquely hands-on approach. His agility as a climber of trees and cliffs is the stuff of legend. Less well known are his many nocturnal excursions to find the roosting places of birds such as tree creepers, pied wagtails, redwings and greylag geese, some of which took on a dual purpose when the BBC put its recording car at his disposal so as to be able to record the dawn chorus.[20] The countless days and nights spent in the field allowed him to develop a huge fund of experiential knowledge that he could draw on for his broadcasts, especially the nature quizzes: Arnold took every question in his stride, delivering his answers without a moment's hesitation. Through the medium of radio he could share his discoveries, insights and enthusiasms with a large audience, inspiring children and adults alike to take an interest in the natural world. That he achieved this through the spoken medium alone, without the aid of the moving images the

---

19 Philip Doughty, letter to Michael Benington, 16 September 1996

20 Arnold preferred to complement his broadcasts with recordings of bird calls made on location, as opposed to recordings of the same species made elsewhere by bird sound specialists like Ludwig Koch. For Arnold's BBC colleagues, such expeditions could be both time-consuming and fruitless. After some debate at the highest level of the BBC, the recording car was eventually grounded.

TV generation would rely on, is a mark of his charismatic personality.

As to what motivated him, whilst adventure, camaraderie and the prospect of one of his wife Jeannette's delicious home-cooked meals awaiting his return all played their part, those who knew him well appreciated that these were underpinned by a profound respect for wild creatures and their habitats. Equipped with keen eyes and a perennially curious mind, he never lost his Quaker-influenced sense of wonder at the myriad complex inter-relationships that sustain life on earth. For Arnold, the sheer diversity and urgency of creation were proof (if such were needed) of God's existence.

That Arnold's legacy continues to this day is borne out by the continuing involvement of family members with nature conservation in the province – from Michael Benington's wildlife paintings and RSPB work, to great grandson Patrick Osborough's volunteering for the Wildfowl & Wetlands Trust. Immediate family aside, however, there is still a very active Observatory on the Copelands with groups of enthusiasts engaged in the ringing of birds. In June 2003 they trapped a manx shearwater that was first ringed, most probably by Arnold, fifty years earlier, making it the oldest bird ever encountered in the British ringing scheme. My grandfather would have been enthralled by such a tangible demonstration of longevity, on the part both of the bird as well as the dedicated Copeland volunteers!

Unknown photographer, Arnold Benington and 'Mayes', Island Magee, 1931

Acknowledgements

Grateful thanks are due to the following for providing access to source materials and giving permission to publish from them: the BBC Written Archives Centre, Caversham; the Belfast Newsletter; National Museums Northern Ireland; and Friends School, Lisburn.

The funding of this publication was made possible by the A. E. Harvey Charitable Trust, Jenny and Peter Osborough, James McDonough, Ian Benington, Kenny Benington and Jane Benington.

James Orr, Director of The Wildfowl & Wetlands Trust's Castle Espie centre, very kindly agreed to host the launch of the book.

Christopher Benington acted as temporary guardian of the field diaries from 1990. Arnold Benington's daughter, Jennifer Osborough provided most helpful comments on the first draft of the manuscript, whilst her brother Michael Benington sourced many of the archival images and gave permission to reproduce his own paintings and drawings.

Much of the fun of preparing this book has come from the knowledge that it is willed into existence by the whole Benington family: Arnold's other grandchildren, Andrew, Fiona, Jessica and Alex, as well as great grandchildren Sophie, Matthew, Emily, Tara, Patrick, Conor, Laughlan, Charis, Amelie and Ava.

Further information

BBC Children's Hour:
www.bbc.co.uk/northernireland/childrenshour/index.shtml

BBC Written Archives Centre:
www.bbc.co.uk/historyofthebbc/contacts/wac.shtml

Birding in Iceland:
www.birdingiceland.com

Copeland Bird Observatory:
www.habitas.org.uk/cbo

National Museums Northern Ireland:
www.nmni.com

Rathlin Island:
www.raghery.com

RSPB in Northern Ireland:
www.rspb.org.uk/northernireland

Wildfowl & Wetlands Trust in Northern Ireland:
www.wwt.org.uk/visit/castleespie

Unknown photographer, Arnold and gyr falcon nestlings, 1955

Chronology

25 April 1903
Birth of J. Arnold Benington at Brookfield near Moira, where his father Charles is Headmaster of a Quaker school

1919
Begins the first of what will eventually extend to 28 volumes of field diaries

1920/22/23/26/27
Holidays in Arnside, Lancashire

February 1921
Spots Glossy Ibis near Lough Neagh

1922
First of many visits to Rathlin Island off the Antrim coast

1926
Gains B.Sc. in Chemistry from Queen's University, Belfast; acquires a Douglas motor-bike

1926-27
First teaching job, at Kempsey House near Worcester

1927-68
Teaches Chemistry and later Biology at Friends' School, Lisburn, latterly as Deputy Head

1928
Discovers Pintail nesting on Lough Neagh (only two previous breeding records in Ireland); acquires Triumph motorbike and sidecar

1930
First descent to a Raven's nest, at Cave Hill near Belfast

9 April 1930
Marries Jeannette Armstrong; they will have three children - Michael (born 1933), Jennifer (born 1938) and Fiona (1943-2004)

May 1936
Discovers Gadwall nesting on Lough Neagh (only one prior breeding record in Ireland)

August 1938
Vacation course with his brother Crawford at Oxford University, every spare moment being spent in the pursuit of Lepidoptera

15 November 1945
Start of 30-year broadcasting career with the first of many radio talks, 'Birds of the Mournes'

1946-63
Regular, usually monthly appearances on BBC Children's Hour (payment was 5 guineas a programme, rising to 13 guineas in 1963)

18 October 1946
Breaks his ankle while taking part in hockey practice with the boys at Friends School

23 February 1949
Meets Sir Peter Scott for the first time, at the Ulster Museum, with whom he will later correspond and broadcast

9 July 1949
Sighting of first Buzzard in Ireland, on Rathlin Island

1953-59
Contributes 'Nature Notes' to *Ulster Illustrated* magazine, illustrated by Michael Benington

February 1954
A prime mover in the founding of the first bird observatory in Northern Ireland on Lighthouse Island, Copelands, County Down

June 1955
First expedition to Iceland, taking in Lake Myvatn and the lava desert around Hrafnabjorg where he photographs Pinkfeet and Gyr Falcons nesting

April 1960, April 1963 & April 1966
Field trips to Aviemore studying Ospreys and Golden Eagles, travelling by public transport the first two occasions, whilst for the final trip Arnold and Michael had a car at their disposal thanks to Harry Breckenridge.

July 1961
Leads second expedition to Iceland with 11 members of the ornithology class of the Workers' Educational Association (Belfast branch)

1961-67
Writes weekly 'Nature Diary' column for *Belfast Newsletter*, illustrated by Michael Benington

May 1973
Holiday at Flims, Switzerland

December 1973
Jeannette dies

February - May 1974
Stays with his daughter Jennifer and her family in Kenya

December 1975 - February 1976
Stays with his daughter Fiona and her family in Singapore

3 March 1976
BBC Northern Ireland television broadcast, 'In the Town', about watching wildlife in Belfast

November 1980
Marries Jane McCauseland

2 April 1982
Dies

Spring 2006
Article by Michael Benington, 'Early Days in Iceland', *Birds Illustrated*, volume 3, issue 3, pp. 43-7

Summer 2007
Article on Rathlin island by Michael Benington, 'Looking back for a brighter future', *Birds Illustrated*, volume 4, issue 4, pp. 16-20

Right: Arnold Benington, Goldfinch, 1925

Back cover: C.R.L., Homemade get well card sent to Arnold Benington, 1958 (Arnold was affectionately known to his friends as Benny)